ALSO BY
ELLEN ORLEANS

The Butches of Madison County

Can't Keep A Straight Face:
A Lesbian Looks and Laughs at Life

EDITED BY ELLEN ORLEANS

Boulder Voices:
Boulder County
Lesbian, Gay and Bisexual
Citizens Tell Their Stories

WHO CARES IF IT'S A CHOICE?

SNAPPY ANSWERS TO 101 NOSY, INTRUSIVE AND HIGHLY PERSONAL QUESTIONS ABOUT LESBIANS AND GAY MEN

BY
ELLEN ORLEANS

For information contact
Roz Warren, Laugh Lines Press
P.O. Box 259, Bala Cynwyd, PA 19004
610-668-4252

Author's photographs by
Lori Fuller and Julian Orleans

Printed in U.S.A.
Fourth printing 1996

Library of Congress Catalog Card Number 94-076559

Who Cares If It's A Choice? Snappy Answers to 101
Nosy, Intrusive and Highly Personal Questions
About Lesbians and Gay Men

p.   cm

ISBN 0-9632526-4-x

1. Lesbians—Humor
2. Humor—Gay and lesbian life
3. Feminist/Lesbian Studies—Humor
4. Women—Humor

I. Ellen Orleans, 1961-

FOR LAURIE,
WHO ALWAYS HAS
THE RIGHT ANSWER

IF TIME AND SPACE
ARE CURVED,
WHERE DO ALL THE
STRAIGHT PEOPLE
COME FROM?

CONTENTS

ACKNOWLEDGMENTS

There's a running joke amongst my friends: Watch out whenever you tell a funny story, because it might end up in one of Ellen's books.

But for *Who Cares If It's a Choice?*, I didn't merely eavesdrop on conversations; I sought out friends and cohorts in a deliberate quest for ideas and answers. Their responses helped shape this book.

So thanks to Verna, who back in 1989 asked me the very first question for which I had a snappy answer. And to Sam, Tammi, and Jim for keeping me abreast of queer cutting edges. To Steve and Mike for sharing insights *and* intimate details of their lives. (I loved getting e-mail about penis piercing!)

Thanks to friends in cyberspace who shared their outrageous questions: Laura Antoniou (editor of *Leatherwomen*), Peter Holden, JoniPony (on the difference between a dildo and a penis), Tracy Schmidt (on bi ignorance) and Glenna Tallman.

Also, thanks to Lynne Yamaguchi Fletcher whose book, *The First Gay Pope and Other Records* was a wonderful source of information, as was Eric Marcus's *Is It A Choice?*

Emotionally wiped out by Amendment Two, my spiritual being was renewed by Dorothy Allison and Essex Hemphill at CU's Gay and Lesbian Studies Conference. I thank these writers for living lives of honesty and courage.

Gratitude also goes to Diane DiMassa, Stacy Sheehan, Suzanne Westenhoefer, Ron Romanovsky, Paul Phillips, Alison Bechdel, Rita Mae Brown, Kate Clinton, Carrie Dearborn, Brandie Erisman, Marga Gomez, Nikki Gosch and Deirdre Smith, Lorraine Hutchins, Jim Marks, Dr. Meg Moritz, Nina Paley, Carol Seajay, Noreen Stevens and Karen Williams — all of whom offered me support and encouragement.

On a brass tacks level, Lori Fuller assisted with photography, editing and late night counseling, proving once again that there *is* life after a break-up. Richard Smith pitched in with proofreading and his fax machine; Roz Warren offered faith and her East Coast sense of humor.

And finally, my unabashed love (yeah, yeah, yeah) to Laurie, who not only believes in my writing; but has backed up her assertions with proofreading, free food and expert managerial advice.

INTRODUCTION

Coming Out: what a gut-wrenching experience. How can you explain your new-found homosexuality to your loved ones when you still have your own questions? How can heterosexual people accept a loved one's gay identity when they've been brainwashed—I mean socialized—to believe it's an unnatural abomination?

The answer? It's in your hands. Yes, this book is the perfect choice for everyone wanting to understand the gay lifestyle. So, before coming out to your parents, prepare them with this book. And by all means share it with guidance counselors, county social workers, your boss at work, your minister—

Wait!!! I'm kidding! (I may be a humorist but I'm not a sadist.) This is a *parody* book. It isn't serious. In fact, it's packed with lies. I should know. I wrote them.

Ah, homosexuality: the current darling of pseudo-scientists, lifestyle reporters and anthropological-wannabees. With this new found fame, has come an onslaught of question and answer books, articles and pamphlets.

If, however, you've grown beyond the "Are gay people normal?" stage or have had it with the "We're just like you!" attitude (and who is the "you" that we are just like, may I ask?), then consider this book your personal "het ignorance neutralizer." Share it with your queer pals. Explain the in-jokes to your well-meaning straight friends.

As much as I delight in writing humor, I find that it often poses dilemmas. For instance, knowing that a mother in Virginia has legally abducted the son of her lesbian daughter, how can I turn around and write parodies about parents accepting their gay children?

Still, I believe in humor. I believe in its power; especially in its subversive power. Humor creeps in undetected, going places where a heavy-handed approach cannot.

Besides, I have my own scientific theory about humor. I believe that when people laugh, the blood vessels in their brains enlarge, making them, in effect, more open-minded. It is during this instant of open-mindedness that we can sneak in and place a small piece of information into the cerebrum. It might be a simple message, like "Discrimination is Bad." Or something more complex, such as "Lesbians and gays make good parents." Or possibly, "Homosexuals should be compensated for injustice done to them with very large refunds from the IRS."

Doris Lessing said, "Laughter is by definition healthy." Here's to your health!

Ellen Orleans
Boulder, Colorado
April 1994

WHO CARES IF IT'S A CHOICE?

1

GETTING STARTED

■ **Where did the word lesbian come from?**

Roughly translated from the Greek, lesbian means "lover of wet sex."

■ **Really?**

No, not really. Actually, over 2,500 years ago, a woman-loving poet named Sappho lived and wrote on the Greek island of Lesbos, hence the word "lesbian." While many lesbians are familiar with Sappho and Lesbos, what is less often known is that during this same period over a dozen such "training ground" islands existed throughout the world. Hundreds of artifacts sharing common subject matter have been found on these islands, indicating the inhabitants descended from a single, mighty tribe. Among the objects found were statues of smiling, large-breasted women with big thighs and bellies, ceremonial masks with pierced noses, and petrified sandals that bear an uncanny resemblance to Birkenstocks.

■ **What is a homosexual man?**

A homosexual man is someone who is so incredibly closeted, so profoundly insecure, and so barely able to admit that he even has sexual feelings (much less for another man) that he actually uses the dopey word homosexual to describe himself.

Or he is so incredibly *over* all this talk about self-acceptance and self-respect and so into *being* queer, *thinking* queer and *breathing* queer that it's precisely because he finds the word "ho-mo-sex-u-al" so unbelievably dumb that he wears it on his T-shirt.

■ **What is the difference between a lesbian and a dyke?**

About $30,000 per year.

Actually, this is a line by comic Lea Delaria. Now if she could only explain the difference between a dyke, a bulldyke and a bulldagger.

■ Are there different kinds of lesbians?

Yes! A few of the categories include

- "Protest, Boycott and March" radical dykes
- feminist-theory, process-or-die lesbians
- Rugby/softball/all-around jock lesbians (and the women who pamper them)
- Earth-Mother/Mother-Earth, pagan lesbians
- Old-time, pack-a-day, bar lesbians
- "we're just like you, we don't want to offend anyone" lesbians
- "we're *nothing* like you, we want to offend everyone" lesbians

■ Are there different kinds of gay men?

Yes, gay men also come in a variety of makes and models. A small sampling:

- Country-western gays (and those who merely dress like them)
- White picket fence homosexuals
- Young, hip and oh-so-queer dance club fags
- Corporate activists/corporate closet cases
- Frat boy look-alikes
- Homophobic by day/cruising boys by night
- Ordinary by day/ flaming queens by night

■ Are lesbians and gays born that way?

No, we are conceived that way. Consider it an act of divine intervention.

■ How do you become a homosexual?

Well, first there's the talent competition, then evening wear, and of course the all-important swimsuit competition.

Okay—this is not a *real* answer. It's actually a joke by popular lesbian comic Suzanne Westenhoefer.

The truth? Well, first there's the general aptitude test, then there's the spatial relations section, then the all important test of eye-hand coordination.

■ Does just one homosexual experience make you lesbian or gay?

Absolutely. In fact, if you've even had so much as a homosexual thought, you're automatically lesbian or gay. So if you have had any homosexual experiences, as dull or non-stimulating as they might have been, turn yourself in to your nearest gay or lesbian center and register immediately. Your gay I.D. will be sent to you within 10 working days.

If you are a man, during this ten day waiting period you must buy a health club membership and redecorate your house. If you are a woman, you must purchase at least $200 worth of lesbian-themed books and one or more cats.

Questions? Call 1-800- I'M QUEER.

■ At what age do you know that you're homosexual?

As you might imagine, this varies greatly. Guys seem to be aware of their sexuality early on. A single erection while watching Batman free Robin from the clutches of the Riddler provided many young men with their first clue. One gay friend told me that his childhood role models were Bert and Ernie. For others, it was Skipper and Gilligan.

Women seem to discover their sexual orientation more from personal experiences. Although I didn't realize it at the time, my first clue was when I zipped up Bobby Wolinsky's fly for him in the second grade. My teacher said this was not proper—that that was a boy's *private* area. At the time, I didn't see what the big deal was. Guess I still don't.

■ Is being homosexual natural?

Not only that, but for lesbians it's often organic.

■ If someone tells you that they're homosexual, what should you do?

Knowing the appropriate response is crucial, although it, of course, varies according to your relationship with the homosexual in question.

For instance, if you are the mother or father of this person, your response should be as follows:

1. Open your mouth and stand there in wordless horror.

2. After 15 seconds of this, break out in uncontrollable sobs, which should last at least a half hour. (Note: this action is only for the mother. The father should continue the wordless horror, punctuated only by occasional grunts.)

Another Note: If you are the teenage brother of the declared homosexual, make a face and say "Gross." Then forget about it and ask to borrow the car.

If you are the younger tomboy sister, say "Cool. Can I meet your friends?"

3. Mother and father should chase siblings out of the room, then turn on each other, hurling accusations.

Sample accusations:
I *told* you to play catch with him more often.
I *warned* you not to dress her in that powder blue snow suit.

4. Make emergency appointment with psychiatrist, declaring you'll pay for as many visits as it takes to make your child normal again.

5. After the first meeting with the psychiatrist, vow to never return, having been told that your child is fine, and *you* are ones that need to adjust.

6. Tossing aside the P-FLAG phone number your child gave you, promise to cut off all communication forever.

7. Call two days later, pretending it never happened.

8. After a brief waiting period (anywhere from two weeks to twenty years) dig up the P-FLAG phone number and call it. Find out that your next door neighbor is president of the local chapter.

9. Attend your first P-FLAG meeting.

10. Discover your true calling in life.

11. Phone your child and tearfully proclaim, "You are my child. I love you unconditionally, just the way you are!"

12. At Thanksgiving dinner, after three glasses of wine, start telling stories about great aunt Edna and her "friend" Sonya.

13. Begin nagging your child to find someone special and settle down.

■ **How do you know if you are lesbian or gay?**

Please consult the handy flow charts on the following pages.

■ **Aren't gay people the result of domineering mothers and passive fathers?**

No, they are the result of passive *mothers* and domineering *fathers*. No, wait—I think that's hyperactive sisters and passive-aggressive brothers. . .or possibly the result of sluggish cousins. What the hell, let's blame it on the family dog.

■ **Is homosexuality a mental illness?**

No, but homophobia is.

MEN, FOLLOW THIS HANDY FLOW CHART TO FIND OUT!

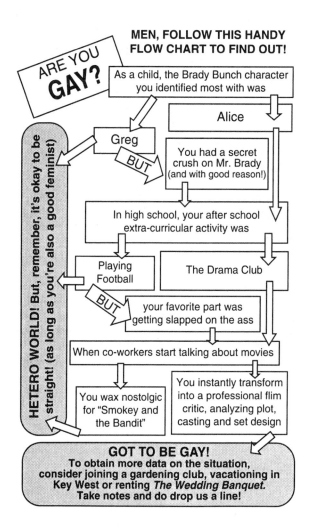

ARE YOU GAY?

As a child, the Brady Bunch character you identified most with was

Alice

Greg

BUT

You had a secret crush on Mr. Brady (and with good reason!)

In high school, your after school extra-curricular activity was

Playing Football

The Drama Club

BUT

your favorite part was getting slapped on the ass

When co-workers start talking about movies

You wax nostolgic for "Smokey and the Bandit"

You instantly transform into a professional flim critic, analyzing plot, casting and set design

HETERO WORLD! But, remember, it's okay to be straight! (as long as you're also a good feminist)

GOT TO BE GAY!
To obtain more data on the situation, consider joining a gardening club, vacationing in Key West or renting *The Wedding Banquet.*
Take notes and do drop us a line!

25

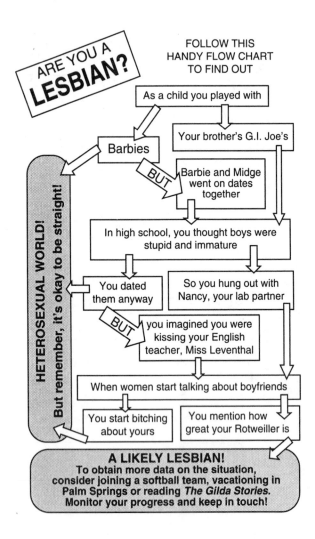

ARE YOU A **LESBIAN?**

FOLLOW THIS HANDY FLOW CHART TO FIND OUT

As a child you played with

Your brother's G.I. Joe's

Barbies

BUT Barbie and Midge went on dates together

In high school, you thought boys were stupid and immature

You dated them anyway

So you hung out with Nancy, your lab partner

BUT you imagined you were kissing your English teacher, Miss Leventhal

When women start talking about boyfriends

You start bitching about yours

You mention how great your Rotweiller is

HETEROSEXUAL WORLD! But remember, it's okay to be straight!

A LIKELY LESBIAN!
To obtain more data on the situation, consider joining a softball team, vacationing in Palm Springs or reading *The Gilda Stories*. Monitor your progress and keep in touch!

26

■ **Are most gay men militant homosexuals? Or is that a stereotype?**

It's a stereotype; albeit a refreshing one. At the 1993 National Gay and Lesbian Task Force conference, gay men voted 3 to 1 to revise the official national gay male stereotype from "sissified pansy" to "militant homosexual."

The official *dyke* stereotype is still unratified; it's toss-up between "political activist do-gooder" and "chic trendsetter." Lesbians have yet to reach consensus on the issue.

■ **Is the stereotype about ice-pick wielding, revenge-seeking maniac lesbians true?**

Yes, so watch out!

■ **I am white and I recently met a black woman who told me she was a lesbian. Are all black people gay?**

This is a real question. I attended an Unlearning Racism workshop where an African-American lesbian said she'd actually been asked this! No, not all black people are gay. This question can't help but make one wonder, however, "Are all white people this stupid?"

■ **What is the homosexual agenda?**

The homosexual agenda is a figment of the religious right's imagination. As performers Ron Romanovsky and Paul Phillips say, "They're always talking about the homosexual *agenda*. . . as if queers could agree on *anything*. We can't even decide what to call ourselves."

■ **I am a woman who likes to dress like a lesbian, go dancing with lesbians, gossip about lesbians and argue queer politics. The only problem is that I'm not sexually attracted to women, not even a little. Can I be a "straight lesbian"?**

No. You can be supportive of lesbians, you can enjoy lesbian culture, you can be a feminist, a bohemian, left bank, counter-culture, avant-garde, and completely hip, smart and trendy, but you *cannot* be a straight lesbian.

■ **Why do lesbians want to look like men?**

We like to tease straight women.

■ **Can you be seduced into being gay?**

Is that an offer?

2

IN THE LIFE
LANGUAGE, SYMBOLS AND RITUALS OF THE QUEER NATION

■ **What does "being in the closet" mean?**

Well, for starters, if you can actually be in your closet, you must have one of those big walk-in kinds, one in which you can move about without tripping over your shoes or being poked in the eye by hangers. Still, no matter how large a closet you have, after a while it becomes an uncomfortable and stuffy place to be. Kind of like keeping your sexual orientation a secret.

■ **What are "code words"?**

Code words are a discreet way of stating "she's a lesbian" or "he's gay" without actually saying it. While some straight people may be aware of the implication of terms such as "a friend of Dorothy's," "musical" and "Lebanese," few know the hidden meaning of phrases like "Looks like rain," "A half pound of Swiss, please" and "I'd like a receipt."

■ **What is "The Gay Lifestyle"?**

I think it was a 1938 movie with Ginger Rogers and Fred Astaire.

■ **What is the significance of the color purple in gay culture?**

Purple is the color of royalty, supporting the popular theory that homosexuals descend from a long line of nobility.

■ **What is the meaning of the rainbow flag?**

The rainbow flag represents the concept that gay, lesbian and bi communities are composed of people from all backgrounds and experiences. Now if we could all work as closely together as the stripes in the flag, we'd really get somewhere. . . .

■ **What are freedom rings?**

A few years back, a gay graphic designer was working on a logo for the Gay Games. His lover called and while they chatted on the phone about redecorating their bathroom, the designer idly played with some colored paper clips on his desk. As the discussion turned into a heated debate over floor tiles, he began twisting and mangling the paper clips. By the time the phone call ended (they decided on basic eggshell with a mint green accent throw rug), our gay friend noticed that the paper clips looked like both the symbol for the Heterosexual Olympics and the gay rainbow flag.

Working with Shocking Grey, (an upscale gay mail order catalog) he developed "freedom rings"— six anodized aluminum rings, each a color of the rainbow, generally worn around the neck. Produced at a manufacturing cost of 83¢ for the set, freedom rings retail for $8 to $10. No hip queer should be seen without them.

■ **What does wearing a pinky ring mean?**

Wear one to Provincetown next summer and you'll find out.

■ **What about Doc Martens, Birkenstocks, bolo ties, pierced noses, triple-pierced ears and skinny ties? Aren't these gay symbols as well?**

They used to be, but they were appropriated by the mainstream. This phenomenon reminds me of a code word used to describe lesbians: "advanced," which correctly suggests that lesbians and gay men are trendsetters.

Don't believe it? Consider this: the mainstream is *still* having an orgy with the term "PC." Lesbians not only originated "Politically Correct," but also processed through it way, way, back—when Meg was still touring, Holly had short hair, and Tracy Chapman was just a warm up act for Cris.

Gay men created disco and black gay men in particular introduced snapping and voguing. Madonna merely got rich off of it.

And back in 1985, JoAnn Loulan was already talking about codependency and healing the inner child. Straight folks? *They* were still mucking around with the "Cinderella Complex."

And let's give credit to leather dykes. For years they took their stand with leather pants, vests and jackets. Then suddenly, boom! Leather is everywhere—from trendy boutiques to Montgomery

Ward. Women who cringe at the word lesbian are now slaves to a trend *we* started.

What else are lesbians and gays responsible for? Early cave drawings, movable type, surfing, the discovery of fire *and* electricity, Haiku, Federal Express, aluminum siding, polyester fabrics (although we don't like to admit to that one), the food processor, indoor swimming pools, remote control and waterproof mascara. By the way, we also landed on the moon in 1953.

■ **Why do some lesbians, bisexuals and gay men use the word "queer" to describe themselves?**

Because it's a whole lot simpler to say "queer community" than "lesbian, bisexual and gay community." Not to mention, "lesbian, bisexual, gay and transgendered community." We're activists and we don't have time to mess around with long, awkward terminology.

■ What does the term "straight" mean?

It's kind of like the word "square" but not as derogatory. According to some sources, it derived from the description of the placement of the male and female body during heterosexual sex.

■ What is a sweater fag?

A sweater fag is gay man who'll spend $90 on a sweater from Saks Fifth Avenue in order to attract other men, then decline to have sex with them because "it's too messy."

As you might guess, you won't find a sweater fag attending meetings of his local Queer Nation chapter.

■ What is a "queen"?

A queen is a gay man with an eccentric mix of attitude, flair, self-absorption and charm. There are all sorts of queens out there. Some examples:

Control Queen: imagine a type-A Virgo with PMS that never goes away.

Size Queen: obsession with male endowment (and I don't mean financial bequests).

Closet Queen: No, it's not a clothing fixation. A closet queen is so fanatic about keeping his homosexuality a secret that he fails to notice that everyone else figured it out years ago.

REAL LIFE
RESTROOM DRAMA!!

A Service of Our "Quick Comebacks to
Memorize Ahead of Time" Department

Like so many lesbians, do you wrestle over the ever-present problem of being mistaken for a man in a public restroom? Have you always wanted to answer with a smart retort but have never known what to say?

As a public service, two fearless lesbians, Glenna Tallman and Laura Antoniou, share their experiences and wisdom with us:

> Bald from radiation treatments, I was in an airport restroom when a very foxy and pert woman asked me if I was in the wrong bathroom. I simply pulled down the top of my sweat pants and said, "I sure don't think so, but you'd be very welcome to check it out!"

> While I was in the bathroom at work, a co-worker decided to embarrass me and a friend of mine by mentioning loudly (to no one in particular), "I thought I was in the *women's* room."

> My friend replied, "No, it's the lesbian steal-a-woman meeting center! And we're so glad you could make it!"

■ **What is "outing"?**

"Outing" is when you promote gay pride and visibility by publicly announcing that a famous person (who is earnestly hiding his or her sexual orientation) is queer, thus producing an angry, ashamed and fearful role model for gay youth everywhere. Still, when the target is a massively anti-gay senator who's being cruising boys in bars for years, outing can be irresistibly satisfying.

■ **When reporting about a newly-discovered lesbian or gay man, what is the proper adjective to use before the word "homosexual"?**

If you're writing about a prestigious Cardinal in the Catholic church who's been denouncing gays as "perverted abominations" for decades, the proper adjective is "confessed" homosexual.

Use the term "admitted" homosexual for a big Hollywood star who's faked a string of marriages to the opposite sex. "Avowed" homosexual is appropriate for an eminent Republican who just got plain sick of leaving his boyfriend at home during all those $1000-a-plate fund raisers.

■ Do lesbians and gay men recruit people into being gay?

Yes, although we don't have to work at it nearly as hard as the Army does. Generally, we just circulate flyers which read something like this:

BE GAY!

Join the ranks of creative and intriguing people such as Michelangelo, Shakespeare and Melissa Etheridge.

Women!
You don't have to spend the rest of your life fooling around with make-up and panty hose.

Men!
Now you can have that long-awaited opportunity to fool around with make-up and panty hose!

Be part of a group of deep-thinking risk-takers who have broken away from society's confining roles and dared to examine the fullest of human potential.

IN OTHER WORDS
BE ALL THAT YOU CAN BE

■ How do gay people recognize each other?

Just like seasoned CIA spies, gay people have an intricate system of signs and signals which we use to identify each other. These range from the obvious rainbow flag and pink triangle to the more subtle eye contact maintained for a moment too long and the handshake that doesn't let go right away.

Other signs are pinky rings, labryses and double women symbols for the gals and Cartier rolling rings and pierced right ears (or is it left ears?) for the guys.

There are dozens of other symbols as well, but under the lesbian loyalty oath, I'm sworn to secrecy and cannot reveal them.

■ Where do most lesbians live?

In bed—during the first few months of the relationship, at least.

Seriously though, 90% of all lesbians live on huge tracts of secluded womyn's land in 23 different states, where they train for the eventual overthrow of the government. The number of lesbians on womyn's land is approximately 60,000,000 or roughly half the entire female population of the U.S.

An additional 1.2 million are scattered across cities, suburbs and small towns, where—in order to confuse the religious right—they pose as urban chic, militant queer upstarts, girls next door and kindly spinsters sharing a house. The situation is similar in most countries around the world.

■ Where do most gay men live?

In saunas. . .

Gotcha! Just joking again. Actually, most gay men live in West Hollywood where they clandestinely meet to write, direct and act in propaganda films, which will be used to soothe the masses after the lesbian overthrow of the country. See above.

■ I get it. It's a joke about a gay takeover. Right? RIGHT?! Umm, what I was wondering was if there are any particular cities or towns where gays live.

Lesbians and gays can be found in all cities and towns, although some popular spots are the Castro and Mission District in San Francisco, West Hollywood outside Los Angeles, Cheesman Park in Denver, Montrose in Houston, West Greenwich Village in New York City, Jamaica Plain in Boston, Northampton, Massachusetts. . .the list goes on and on. And—oh yeah!—right next door to you!

■ What's the story behind lesbian potlucks?

Potlucks first cropped up as a way to free lesbians from the ominous role of "hostess"—a duty formerly thrust upon them by ambitious, big business husbands who would later leave them for younger women. With everyone pitching in food and their own place setting, no one got stuck cooking all day or washing dishes until midnight.

Potluck dishes later evolved into stereotypical, macrobiotic casseroles featuring bulgar, seaweed and an indistinct root vegetable. As the lesbian nation matured, many women became bold enough to bring a bucket of Kentucky Fried, bravely defying stares of contempt and disbelief.

Of late, many dykes are simply meeting over decaf at lesbian-owned cappuchino bars. The art of the potluck has not been lost, however. In many parts, gay men have taken it up and their cooking is just fabulous.

■ What is a "Mirth and Girth" club?
What is a "bear" contest?

Contrary to all those sleek Adonis-like bodies that have come to represent the essence of the gay male, many gay men are turned on by other looks and body shapes. A "mirth and girth" society promotes and admires large and fat men; fans of "bears" celebrate profuse body and facial hair. A gay sub-culture has emerged around these phenomena— including clubs, publications and contests.

According to one story, a gay man in New York City won a bear contest and put the trophy in his home. His mother was visiting one day, saw the trophy and asked about it. A bit reluctant at first, he explained about the contest. Unfazed, she listened to his explanation, and had only one question, "So. . . how much money did you win?"

By the way, there are admiration societies for large lesbians as well. One California group is named "Girth Mothers."

■ What are Radical Faeries?

Radical Faeries are sometimes identified as proto-types of ACT-UP activists. While both work for social justice through civil disobedience and public protest, the two groups can be distinguished from each other by their dissimilar facial hair styles. Also, Radical Faeries prefer flowing skirts to intentionally ripped jeans. Incidentally, rumors that the Radical Faeries began Log Cabin Clubs as a way to infiltrate the Republican Party are purely conjecture.

■ What is a gay bar like?

Well, before you can even walk in, you have to show your gay I.D. (Remember, it must be signed by two witnesses and include the year you came out.) The moment you get past the bouncer, 300 pairs of eyes will stare you down, deciding—with one shared mind—if you are a real homosexual or merely an imposter taking notes for a grad school thesis.

Now if it's a smaller bar in a smaller town, there might be 30 pairs of eyes instead of 300. And you'll know exactly who each of those eyeballs belong to: someone you slept with last month whose name you can't remember, an old boyfriend who's kissing your therapist, half your rugby team and of course the ex-lover you've come here to forget.

■ What is NGLTF, HRCF, and GLA?

R U confused 2? Well, what is the gay liberation movement if not one big acronym? NGLTF, the National Gay and Lesbian Task Force is best known for its hot (if controversial) lesbian leaders. HRCF, The Human Rights Campaign Fund (which recently won the prestigious "Most Closeted Name Award") is noted for running around on Capitol Hill in dresses and jackets and ties (yes, that's the *men* in jackets and the *women* in dresses). Finally, GLA— Gay and Lesbian Americans—is a new group with branch chapters around the country. They haven't been around very long yet, so it's hard to know just how to make fun of them.

■ In a male couple relationship, who takes out the garbage? And who does the cooking, the laundry and the yard work?

Into traditional gender roles are we? Okay, it *is* a legitimate question, and honestly, one whose answer I wasn't sure of myself. So I asked my friends Steve and Mike. They divulged that, in most gay male couples, the decision of who takes out the trash, cleans the toilets, etc., is settled by wrestling in the nude. I had suspected that this was the case, but it was good to have my suspicions confirmed.

■ **What is a "turkey baster baby"?**

Lesbians are so creative that they've leapt way beyond conventional baby making methods. Instead of relying on the usual vehicle for transporting sperm into the uterus, lesbian moms-to-be used to use a turkey baster. So even though syringes are more common these days, the traditional turkey baster designation has stuck.

More interesting perhaps than turkey basters themselves are the various ways in which sperm is procured. Fresh or frozen, anonymous or from a dear trusted friend—figuring out whose sperm to use is perhaps the toughest challenge lesbian parents will ever face.

One popular method is the upwardly-mobile and unbelievably complex sperm banks where you choose a donor based not only on physical appearance, musical ability and favorite hobbies, but also on the answers he gives to required essays such as "Why I Am Donating My Sperm" and "Message to My Future Child."

Move over Alfred Kinsey. . .

IT'S THE
BUTCH/FEMME/NELLIE SCALE

Experiencing a gay identity crisis? Wondering if you're a lipstick lesbian, *lisp*stick drag queen, dyke separatist, queer sistah, bisexual performance artist (is that redundant?) or Republican homosexual?

Plus there's the utter chaos of butch/femme and butch/nellie. Recruiting volunteers to test my "Are You Gay?" flow chart series (see *Getting Started*), I was devastated to find femmes registering as straight and gay men ending up in the lesbian category!

So, in a heartfelt effort to better represent the mind-boggling spectrum of butch/femme/nellie, I have spent over 30 arduous minutes painstakingly developing the following highly scientific quiz. Rest assured, this definitive assessment will provide the final word in measuring this aspect of queer identity.

Please turn the page.

WHAT IS YOUR BUTCH/NELLIE QUOTIENT?

FOR GAY MEN

(Dykes, you've got your own quiz later on!)

Answer these simple questions to determine where you fit on the Butch/Nellie Behavior-Identity Scale

My personal role model(s):

A. Larry Kramer
B. Bob and Rod Jackson-Paris
C. Greg Louganis
D. Barbara Stanwyk

My idea of a Saturday afternoon well spent:

A. Chaining myself to the White House gates while wearing my black leather jacket.

B. Power rototilling the garden after a morning of free weights.

C. Going for a quick romp with the dogs before picking out a new lawn ornament.

D. Watching soap operas while re-labeling the video collection.

The household chore I'm most likely to do:

A. Oiling the chain saw.
B. Fixing the garbage disposal.
C. Programing the VCR.
D. Sweeping thoroughly between the oven and the sink.

RESULTS

Mostly A's – A No Holes Barred Butch!
You blow those swishy stereotypes
right out of the water!

Mostly B's – Nellie Butch
Flexibility is one of your sexiest features.

Mostly C's – Butchy Nellie
You keep everyone guessing
(and that's exactly how you like it)

Mostly D's – A Nellie's Nellie
But that's no surprise to you, girl.

A Mixture of A, B, C and D's
Part of a New Breed: The NeoHomosexual
or: *Wow, you answered honestly!*

BUTCH, FEMME OR IN BETWEEN?
(IT'S A SLIDING SCALE THING)

FOR LESBIANS
(Guys, don't confuse the issue by taking this quiz!)

Choose the answer that most closely matches your personal life experience. Feel free to take time to process before answering.

My Attitude Towards Make-up:
    A. I wear it because I enjoy it. Got a problem with that?

    B. I wear it because it turns my girlfriend on.

    C. I'd wear it on Halloween if I were dressing as a vampire.

    D. I'd possibly consider wearing stage make-up, but only if I were being interviewed for Dyke T.V.

High School Experiences:
    A. In Home-Ec I sewed a lavender jumpsuit.

    B. In Home-Ec I sewed lavender overalls—and in auto mechanics I rebuilt a small engine.

    C. I was captain of the field hockey team.

    D. I cross-dressed to be on the football team.

My Approach Towards Cooking:

A. I get off on making a better souffle than my gay brother.

B. I believe all people should know how to feed themselves.

C. I cook because it attracts hot femme lovers.

D. Hefting cast iron frying pans builds muscle definition.

RESULTS

Mostly A's – Femme Mystique
Joan Nestle is your personal savior

Mostly B's – Butchy Femme
Butch in the streets; femme in the sheets

Mostly C's – Femmey Butch
Elusive and in charge!

Mostly D's – Butch's Butch!
*Enough of these dumb quizzes—
where's my power drill?*

**A Mixture of A, B, C and D's
Don't Label Me, Sister!**
or: *What are you—a pawn of the patriarchy?*

3

ARTS AND LEISURE

■ What is "Claire of the Moon"?

Released in 1992, *Claire of the Moon* is the non-lesbian lesbian movie that won't die. The film is set at an Oregon writing retreat, where a half-dozen Caucasian female stereotypes gather to process, bitch and play with their sexual energies.

The apparent purpose of this film is to torture large numbers of lesbians, who spend two and a half hours waiting for Noel and Claire to "do it." Until the last 15 minutes, every semi-sexual act in the movie (except for the het ones) is either a near miss or an over-active daydream.

In the theater where I saw the film, this "no, not yet" set-up led one woman to finally cry out, "Oh my god—this is like a bad date!!" This admission was greeted with robust applause from the audience, who then knew they were not alone in their feelings of tedium and frustration.

At one point, I turned to my friend Carol and commented, "The women at this so-called writing retreat aren't getting very much writing done."

"They're doing a better job than whoever wrote this script," she replied.

Despite its stiff acting and contrived situation, the Claire phenomenon continues to grow. Now available from your local lesbian bookstore—

Claire of the Moon: The Video
Claire of the Moon: The Book
Moments: The Making of *Claire of the Moon*
Music from Claire of the Moon: The CD
Writing Claire of the Moon: The Action Video.

Not to mention the *Claire of the Moon* Whiskey, Cigar and Backgammon Set; and *Claire of the Moon* Breakfast Cereal (doesn't snap, crackle or pop; just sits there wilting in the bowl.)

■ What is "Dykes to Watch Out For"?

If it weren't for *Dykes to Watch Out For*, most lesbians would never even bother picking up all those otherwise gay male rags. Drawn by cartoon goddess Alison Bechdel, *Dykes* had millions of lesbians drooling in anticipation of Mo's affair with Thea, betting the rent money on the gender of Clarice and Toni's baby and signing up for the Lesbian Avengers so they could be like Lois and wear a "We Recruit!" T-shirt. Revered by hordes of adoring fans, Alison Bechdel has actually gotten to the point of (gasp!) earning her living as a lesbian cartoonist.

■ Is there a gay male equivalent of "Dykes to Watch Out For" ?

Yes. Drawn by Allen Botchdel, "Dicks to Watch Out For" follows the adventures of four phallic fellows— Peter, Dick, Rod and Willy—as they debate impotence issues, attend circumcision support groups and compare condom styles. "Dicks" hasn't yet reached the quality of "Dykes," but it's a start.

■ What is Hothead Paisan?

Chopping off penises before it was in vogue, cartoon character Hothead Paisan (created by Diane Dimassa) is one of the hottest comics in the nation. Walking around with anything from a Howitzer, bundle of dynamite or hedge shears in her back pocket, the over-caffeinated and under-nourished Hothead mows down, blows up or hacks away all sexist males foolish enough to cross her path. Hothead's fanatical followers are rivaled in numbers only by those of Chicken, her sage-like cat. Hothead Paisan is every pacifist's worst nightmare. And favorite wet dream.

■ What is Daughters of Bilitis?
What is the Mattachine Society?

Before Queer Nation, lesbian-feminism or even the Gay Liberation Front, there were gay and lesbian activist organizations. Gay men began the Mattachine Society; lesbians founded Daughters of Bilitis.

While DOB's stated purpose—the "integration of the homosexual through education of the variant and the public" may seem a tad removed from today's goals, other issues sound more familiar.

In the "Letters to the Editor" column of DOB's newsletter, incensed readers wrote about lesbian marriage, butch-femme and the indifference of homosexual men. Some things never change.

■ **What is *Off Our Backs*?**
What is *On Our Backs*?

They are both magazines. *Off Our Backs* is radical politics, social commentary and the heated exchange of opinions. *On Our Backs* is sex, sex, and sex. Guess which one is glossy and which is newsprint.

■ **What is *OutLook*?**

OutLook was a socially responsible, intelligent and innovative magazine, presenting a balanced view of lesbian and gay issues while accepting neither alcohol nor sex-line advertising. No wonder it went under.

■ **Who is Rita Mae Brown?**

While many people think of Rita Mae Brown as the author of the lesbian-positive, ground breaking book, *Rubyfruit Jungle*, few know that "Rita Mae Brown" is actually the pseudonym of Rhonda Marie Beige, a happily-married, straight mother of four who has absolutely no interest in cats, horses or Greek mythology. "Ms. Brown" lives in a split-level house in a Northern Indiana suburb.

She penned her first two books *Freshly Mowed Lawn* and *Predictable Life* on a card table in her rec room. They were both publishing flops. At the suggestion of her editor, she tried writing from the viewpoint of a lesbian from the South. The rest, as they say, is herstory.

■ What is Naiad Press?

The largest lesbian publisher in the country, Naiad Press's romance/adventure/mystery books are often snubbed by haughty lesbian highbrows. However, if you look carefully behind that snooty lesbian's copy of "The Journal of Theoretical Lesbian Thought," you'll see she's *really* reading *Murder in a Lesbian Love Nest.*

■ What is "women's music"?

Developed in the early 1970's, "women's music" is this weird, ambiguous term for "lesbian music," although the word lesbian doesn't show up much in the lyrics.

The early performers in this genre—the Trinity of Meg , Cris and Holly—became demi-gods (or is that demi-goddesses?) , worshipped by masses of mostly white women who rejected high heels and eye liner in favor of denim shirts and blue jeans. These women became known as the tribe of Olivia, and vowed to transform the planet by returning to the land, foregoing meat and learning to play acoustic guitar.

But that was 20 years ago. Today, followers of Olivia make their pilgrimages on cruise ships. Times change.

■ What is "Michigan"?

It's a state in the Midwest where they make cars and beer—oh you're probably wondering about the Michigan Womyn's Music Festival. A rite of passage for thousands of lesbians, Michigan festi-goers schlep across the country, divide themselves into categories, set up their tents, take off their clothes, stand in long lines, neglect their work shifts, play volleyball, occasionally mud wrestle, discover their high school math teacher really was "that way," attend workshops, go shopping, and even get to hear a few concerts.

■ **What is the Dinah Shore Golf Classic?**

The Dinah Shore Golf Classic is the upwardly-mobile version of the Michigan Womyn's Music Festival. Instead of music, there is golf; instead of tents, Bed and Breakfasts; instead of volleyball/mud wrestling, there are large indoor dance parties. And of course, women do not take off their shirts on the golf course.

■ **Do gay men have the equivalent of music festivals?**

Yes, it's called Fire Island.

4

RELIGION

■ **What does the Bible say about homosexuality?**

Love thy neighbor, last time I checked.

■ **But what about Leviticus 18:22?**

Biblical scholars have really missed the boat with this one. The verse, which reads "Thou shalt not lie with a man as with a woman. It is an abomination" is not about same gender sexual relations at all; it is actually about military preparedness.

You see, God (being omnipotent) knows exactly how men lie with women: they hog the bed, steal the sheets and snore. Biblical women put up with this, figuring it was easier than the problems men had to deal with: sacrificing he-goats, not bearing false witness, and keeping track of all those "begats."

However, in conveying Leviticus 18:22, God realized that if—after a long day of smiting Hittites—a couple of exhausted male soldiers fell into a bed together and one grabbed all the covers, the other man clearly would not put up with it. There would be pushing and shoving and drawn swords and you just *know* somebody would get maimed, thus putting yet another soldier out of commission.

So, in order to keep the Israelite army strong, with Leviticus 18:22, God is instructing men to either improve their manners in bed or sleep on the ground.

How any clergyman could derive an anti-gay message out of that simple verse is beyond me.

■ What is MCC?

MCC stands for Metropolitan Community Church, which was founded in 1968 by Troy Perry. While MCC's primary purpose is to create a loving and supportive community for gay Christians, it is also a training ground for gay biblical scholars, who have learned to beat the religious fundamentalists at their own game.

■ **What is Dignity, Integrity and Emergence?**

Initially, I thought Dignity, Integrity and Emergence was a highly-principled law firm, but it turns out I was wrong. Actually, in our unending "crusade" (as it were) to continually confound the Religious Right with our diversity, lesbians and gays have formed a variety of support and worship groups with noble sounding names. To set the record straight, Dignity is Catholic, Integrity is Episcopalian and Emergence is Christian Science.

Incidentally, there is also a national gay Hindu group —Transcendence.

■ **Are there any Jewish gay groups?**

Yes, there are dozens of gay and lesbian synagogues throughout the U.S, giving a whole new spin to the idea of "going to Temple to meet a nice Jewish boy."

5

SOCIAL AND MATING PRACTICES

■ **What kind of sex do lesbians and gay men have?**

Great sex.

■ **Why do lesbians and gay men have great sex?**

First off—we aren't worried about birth control. Also, we are educated about safer sex, and as we all know, safe sex is hot sex. Finally, it takes a lot of perseverance and personal growth to come out as gay or lesbian, acknowledge our homosexuality to others, then find a suitable gay or lesbian lover, all the while dodging homophobia. So when we finally have sex, it's amazing.

■ **Do lesbians and gay men really have great sex, all the time, every time?**

Of course. Would I lie to someone as gullible as you?

■ **What is a "top" ? What is a "bottom"?**

"Top" and "bottom" are sort of like butch and femme, except they don't have the historical context, *and* they apply to both men and women, *and* they don't have the wardrobe considerations. So maybe they really aren't like butch and femme. Perhaps it's clearer to say that they are sex roles: a top is active during sex; a bottom is receptive. Except that sometimes, the bottom really directs the sex act and sometimes the top is on the bottom and a lot of the time the terms are used out of the bedroom wherein "top" is a shortcut for control freak and "bottom" is someone who just goes along for the ride letting the top be into being a top because the bottom knows it's the bottom line that really counts. Hope that clears things up.

■ **What is safer sex?**

Safer sex is when you live in Boston and your lover lives in San Diego.

■ **What does a lesbian bring on the second date?**

A U-Haul.

■ **What does a lesbian bring on the first date?**

Her toothbrush.

■ **A friend told me she was bisexual. I said, "So that means you can only date other bisexuals, right?" She gave me a funny look. Can you explain?**

The reason she gave you that funny look is that bisexual dating rituals are terribly complex. But—in over-simplified terms—bisexual women date in a specific cycle: January, straight men; February—bisexual women; March— bisexual men; April—lesbians. The cycle begins over again in May.

The bisexual male's cycle is a mirror image of the female cycle, with a 45° difference.

■ What is S/M Sex?

You're probably thinking, "Just like straight people, *some* (not all, but *some*) lesbians and gay men enjoy S/M (or sado-masochistic) sex." But what you *don't* know is that in the queer world, S/M stands not for sado-masochistic but for Sweet/Mellow. Had *you* fooled, didn't we?

That's right, gay and lesbian S/M sex usually revolves around bubble baths by candle light, gazing deeply into each others' eyes and giving soothing massages. Occasionally, love making is a part of Sweet/Mellow sex, but often the pair simply falls asleep in each others arms.

So, what about all those people walking around in chaps, harnesses and collars, decked out in nipple rings, whips and chains? Sorry, but they're really not planning to engage in a wild and ferocious sex adventure. More likely they are models for an *Out!* magazine fashion spread. Or maybe they're just planning to surprise Mom and Dad for Sunday dinner.

■ If lesbians like to use dildos, why don't they like penises?

After sex, dildos go back in the drawer.

■ Do all lesbians use dildos?

No. First of all, in order to be allowed to use a dildo, all lesbians must pass the official "I will not confuse my dildo with a penis nor will I secretly fantasize that my female lover is a man" test. Even then, some refuse to use dildos, often for no other reason than that the name is so silly.

■ When lesbians make love, how do they decide who gets to be the man?

While the question of who gets to be the man used to be decided with a simple toss of a coin, things are much more complicated these days. How the question is decided depends largely upon what region of the country one lives in.

In New England, for instance, whoever sleeps on the left side of the bed is the man. And in New York City, the job of being the man goes to the whomever has the rent-controlled apartment.

For the sake of balance, most lesbians alternate this role. For example, in the Plains states, the cycle of "being the man, being the woman" is loosely related to crop rotation; in the Rocky Mountain region it varies according to altitude.

■ **What do gay couples do with each other, anyway?**

If you really can't figure it out—I cringe at the thought of your own sex life.

■ **Okay, I admit it. I have a dull, routine and infrequent sex life. But I still wonder, "What do gay couples do with each other?"**

Anything we want.

■ **When my ex-lover and her current lover break up, how long do I have to wait before I can date my ex-lover's current lover who will then be her ex-lover?**

Homosexual etiquette requires a 24-hour waiting period.

■ **How long do gay and lesbian couples relationships last?**

Forever. Even after a couple breaks up, the relationship goes on and on. Lesbian Thanksgiving dinners prove this fact as they tend to be a conglomeration of ex-lovers, teenage sweethearts and former girlfriends all choosing carefully who they sit next to.

6

SCIENTIFIC WONDERS

■ **What is "gaydar"?**

Gaydar is "gay radar"- an internal sensing device common to gay men and lesbians. While it is most often used "lesbian to lesbian" or "gay man to gay man," it is not uncommon for lesbians to pick out gay men and visa versa.

Many conditions can jam gaydar. Not being out to oneself renders gaydar inoperative and at least one man has noted that bisexuality throws gaydar out of whack.

Some people experience bi-level gaydar. As gaydar expert Peter Holden explains, there is the low-level "yup—there's one" alert and then there's the "OH MY GOD, I want to have your children!" full body electroshock whammy that hits upon eye contact.

For this second level gaydar to occur, not only must both parties' gaydar waves intersect simultaneously, but their hypothalamus glands must also be vibrating at the same frequency.

■ **Why do gay men have better taste in fashion than straight men?**

Surprisingly, the answer is simple: gay men have better fashion taste because they are being judged by other men.

It's similar to the situation faced by straight teenage couples where the female, in order to impress the male, spends hours getting her clothes, hair and makeup just right. The male, knowing that his girlfriend will tolerate his grubby appearance, simply throws on dirty jeans and a Pearl Jam T-shirt.

Obviously, gay guys can't rest on the easy-going female standard of acceptable appearance. They must work diligently to impress each other. It's much tougher than what straight men get by with, but gay men are rewarded for their troubles with great sex.

■ **Why do gay men have cleaner apartments than straight men?**

The explanation to this odd quirk boils down to simple peer pressure, which, by the time a gay man is in his early 20's, has become so ingrown that cleanliness becomes practically instinctual.

When visiting a gay friend and his roommate (yes, it really was his roommate) in their Manhattan apartment several years ago, I sat down to chat in their living room. As we talked, the roommate shifted a vase on the glass table and noticed a ring. He immediately got up, plucked the Windex out of the cupboard, sprayed and wiped the table, replaced the Windex, then sat back down—without a single break in the conversation.

Meanwhile, my friend, who was making himself a bowl of instant oatmeal, noticed that two flakes had landed on the floor. In a single motion, he whipped out the Dustbuster, revved the engine, sucked up the offending flakes, then replaced the unit.

When he noticed that I was staring at both him and his roommate in wide-eyed disbelief, he merely shrugged and said, "We can't help it. We're gay. "

■ Is it true that lesbians walk differently than straight women?

Yes. Lesbians do walk differently than straight women. The absence of panty hose, high heels and a tight skirt are of course a factor, especially in your "screw-the-patriarchy, dress-for-yourself" type lesbian, but it goes beyond that.

Extensive, non-government funded research has shown that all women possess a hormone known as "femirone" which is secreted daily through the pores of the skin. The chemical structure of femirone alters when it comes in continual intimate contact with femirone from other females.

The covalent bonds reorganize into an ionic bond structure, creating a new chemical composition known as "lesbimone."

It is the presence of lesbimone that widens the stride, adds assurance to the step and a sense of purpose to the swinging arms as a dyke strides by.

What is not yet understood is the chemical transformation of lesbimone into "lustimone," a phenomenon that frequently occurs in women's locker rooms, on camping trips and during teenage slumber parties.

■ **Why do some lesbians turn up their collars?**

This was part of a late 1980's fashion statement—as exemplified by Kate Clinton, Heather Bishop, and Chris Cagney—which has since passed. It is not believed to be tied to either DNA or brain waves.

The lesbian tendency to roll up one's sleeves and "get things done" continues—clearly it goes beyond style. Some experts have postulated that this behavior is connected to advanced DNA patterns.

■ **Why are gay people so angry?**

Us? Angry? Hey, *we're* not the ones firing automatic weapons at the Post Office.

■ **I've heard that a disproportionate number of gays and lesbians have homosexual siblings. Does this mean that homosexuality is genetic?**

No, it means it's contagious.

■ **Are there more gay people in the world than there used to be?**

It's true— we *are* increasing exponentially. While some researchers link this phenomenon to anti-oxidants; others attribute it to Lite Beer. Still others say it's just part of the many unexplained scientific wonders of our mysterious world.

8

SOCIOLOGICAL PHENOMENON

■ **Do gay people really make more money than straight people?**

Well, as a matter of fact, yes we do, although not in the way that you think. The truth is that we do literally "make" money; we print it up on cooperatively-owned printing presses.

How can you tell gay money from the regular stuff? Well, it's pretty subtle, of course, but here are some hints. If you hold gay money up to the light, you'll see a slight lavender tinge. Also, the scrollwork in the corners is just a bit more rococo. And if you look very, very carefully, you might notice that the five, ten and twenty dollar dominations bear the portraits of Harvey Milk, Pat Parker and Audre Lorde. The one dollar bill still carries Washington's face, but if you examine it closely, you'll see ol' George is winking at you.

Skeptical? Hey—where do you think the term "queer as a three dollar bill" came from in the first place?

■ Why don't lesbians wear makeup?

Because by the time we finish changing the oil, splitting a cord of firewood, repainting the backyard shed and cleaning the cat box, then *finally* get out to the store to pick some up, the drag queens have bought the place out.

■ Why do drag queens dress like movie stars and Motown vocalists and not ordinary women?

Because drag queens are *queens*—and actresses and singers are the closest things we Americans have to royalty. Your general transvestite, on the other hand, dresses in dozens of ways. Rent Jennie Livingston's video *Paris Is Burning* to learn more.

■ **Is AIDS God's way of punishing gay people?**

No, actually AIDS is God's way of testing straight people for compassion and intelligence in dealing with a pandemic disease. So far, society isn't doing too well.

■ **Why do gay and lesbian people join the military?**

For many of the same reasons that straight people do: as a way to break free of an oppressive family, escape a small hometown or as a last resort for attaining some job skills. A few join believing that they want to serve their country and preserve democracy, but after a few months of blatant military prejudice, that misconception usually dies a quick death.

In addition, homosexuals have unique reasons for joining: young and impressionable men are attracted by the opportunity to accessorize their uniforms with medals and ribbons. And more than a few lesbians like the idea of learning to fly jet bombers and fire assault weapons—skills they can apply later in life when combating homophobia.

■ **Do lesbians have more fun in restaurants than straight people? Or is that just my imagination?**

It's true. Lesbians have more fun than straights because they nibble off each others plates and eat artichokes suggestively. Also, most lesbians play footsie under the table.

Lesbian parents out with their kids, however, have the same amount of fun as straight people out with their kids.

■ **At a party, a gay man walked up to an attractive lesbian and commented, "You're gorgeous. Too bad you're not a man." She threw her drink in his face. Was that remark a social faux pas?**

Yes. The correct comment would have been, "You're gorgeous. Too bad I'm not a lesbian."

9

FINAL QUESTIONS

■ **Why do lesbians have a thing for cats?**

We like surrounding ourselves with peaceful, intelligent and independent beings, who, unlike straight people, aren't always asking us dumb questions about our sexuality.

■ **Are gay people innately funnier than straights?**

We'd like to think so.

■ **Is it true that lesbians and gay men are the product of a superior evolutionary trend?**

Yes!

ADDED BONUS!

THE HETEROSEXUAL QUESTIONNAIRE

1. What do you think caused your heterosexuality?

2. When and how did you decide that you were a heterosexual?

3. To whom have you disclosed your heterosexuality? How did they react?

4. Could it be that your heterosexuality is just a phase?

5. Is it possible your heterosexuality stems from a neurotic fear of others of your same gender?

6. If you have never slept with someone of your same gender, then how do you know you wouldn't prefer it? Isn't it likely that you just haven't met the right same-sex partner yet?

7. Heterosexuals have a history of failures in gay relationships. Do you think you may have turned heterosexual out of fear of rejection?

8. Why do you flaunt your lifestyle with wedding rings, photos at work and talk of your heterosexual escapades?

9. Your heterosexuality doesn't offend me as long as you leave me alone, but why do so many heterosexuals try to seduce others into their orientation?

10. Are cancer, earthquakes and floods God's way of punishing heterosexuals?

11. Considering the battering, abuse and divorce rate associated with heterosexual coupling, why would you want to enter into that kind of relationship?

12. If you should choose to have children, would you want them to be heterosexual, knowing the problems they would face?

13. How can you ever hope to become a whole person if you limit yourself to a compulsive, exclusively heterosexual lifestyle and remain unwilling to explore and develop your normal, healthy, God-given homosexual potential?

14. And anyway, why do heterosexuals place so much emphasis on sex?

Thanks to LABIA (Lesbians and Bisexuals in Association), the women's caucus of Queer Nation/San Francisco who, in 1990, developed some of the questions contained in the Heterosexual Questionnaire.

INDEX

illustration by Noreen Stevens

COLORADO DYKE I.D.

I M 1 2 RU

YEAR CAME OUT: **1985**
VERIFIED BY: **C.Shelton**
          V.Kelly

NOREEN RIVERA WOLINSKY
33 RAD-LES-FEM LANE
BOULDER CO 80306

SEX: **VANILLA** WT: **112** HT. **4'11"**
HAIR: **SHORT** EYES: **FEMME**

X *Noreen Rivera Wolinsky*

OFFICIAL SISTER:
LESBIAN NATION
QUEER COLLECTIVE
DYKE HUMORISTS, INC.

If you liked *Who Cares If It's a Choice?*, you'll love the following essay, excerpted from Ellen Orleans's other book, *Can't Keep a Straight Face*. For information on ordering *Can't Keep a Straight Face and* other women's humor titles, see pages 90–95.

AFFIRMATIONS IN ACTION

A few months back, when I was steeped in despair over my break up, I noticed that I wasn't sleeping well, wasn't eating well, wasn't feeling any enthusiasm for life. Fortunately I still retained the presence of mind to recognize the feelings for what they were: symptoms of depression.

The next week I plopped down on my therapist's couch and announced, "I'm clinically depressed."

"Let's not toss around psychological jargon," she replied. "What are you *feeling*?"

"I'm not hungry. Can't sleep. My self-esteem is shot. What's the purpose in living since we all die anyway?"

"Hmm," she said. "Sound's like you're depressed."

I glared in her direction.

"So, what do you want to do about it?" she asked.

"I want to *wallow* in it," I said, acknowledging that the depression had not dulled my sarcasm.

Of course, I didn't *really* want to wallow in it. But how could I get out of it? My brother was always proclaiming the virtues of affirmations, and I figured I could handle listening to an affirmation tape as long as I kept busy doing something else, like driving or washing dishes.

So, I took myself to the neighborhood New Age store, Healing and Feeling, and asked the clerk if they carried any tapes of loving affirmations for depressed people wallowing through the aftermath of a break up.

"Over there," she said, pointing to the back of the store. Figuring there'd be maybe a dozen tapes of affirmations, I was bowled over to see a whole wall full of them. Louise Hay had two shelves just to herself: *Healing Your Body; Healing Your Mind; Teaching Your Dog to Heal.*

I eyed other titles as well: *Affirmations for the*

Joyous Heart, Six Weeks to Inner Peace, Guided Meditations for the Spiritually Inept, Jane Fonda's Seven Chakra Workout. Nothing seemed right. Besides, at $12.95 each, they were rather pricey. Nothing seemed right. Besides, at $12.95 each, they were rather pricey.

Then I spotted the discount bin. Rummaging through, I found a pile of tapes by T.J. Hay, Louise's lesser-known lesbian sister.

"Now, I'm getting somewhere," I thought, reading the titles. *Getting Clear, Being Queer; The Inner Journey to Coming Out; Affirmations for the Radiant Clitoris.* I finally chose, *Letting Loose of Your Lesbian Ex-Lover.* At $2.99, I knew I'd gotten a deal.

I trotted home, and popped the cassette into the tape player.

"Hello," a warm and kind voice said, "I'm T.J. Hay and together we're going to let loose of your lesbian ex-lover."

I looked at the tape player. "Right." I said.

"Find yourself a comfortable, safe space. Sit down and relax."

"Forget it," I told T.J., "I'm putting away my laundry."

"That's good," the tape said. "Now take a deep breath. And another."

"Whose idea was this?" I muttered, gathering my underwear off the drying rack and putting it the drawer.

"Fine." the tape said, "Now repeat after me, I *love* myself."

"Okay." I told myself, "This was my idea and I can do this." So I repeated after T.J., "I *love* myself."

"I am a *good* person."

"I am basically good," I thought, rolling up a pair of socks. "I am a good person."

"My life is rich and I am blessed."

"Don't push it, T.J.," I thought. But I *said*, "My life is rich and I am blessed."

"I have a loving and forgiving heart."

"I have a loving and forgiving heart," I grumbled, rolling up more socks.

"I love and forgive my ex-girlfriend."

"I love and forgive my ex-girlfriend," I said, choking on my words.

"Except for that incident last winter."

"Except for that incident last winter. . ." Hey, how'd she know about that?

"I'm still pretty ticked off about that."

Damn right. "I *am* still ticked about that."

"In fact, just thinking about it makes me pretty angry."

"*Very* angry." I told the cassette deck.

"In fact, I feel like picking up a soft object and throwing it across the room."

My hand reached out for the alarm clock.

"A soft object," the tape said. "Like a pillow."

I grabbed Ruby, a stuffed red dinosaur that my ex-lover had given me.

"Don't throw that cute dinosaur," the voice said.

"Fine, I'll throw a pair of rolled-up socks."

"How about a sock?" the voice said.

"I'm ahead of you," I told the tape.

"Well then, throw that object."

I heaved the blue and white socks across the room. My cat flew off the bed and ran for the closet, knocking over the drying rack in the process. Clothes spilled to the floor.

"I am really angry," the tape said.

"I am really angry," I said, throwing another pair, pink this time. The socks hit my change dish and coins flew all over.

"Damn, am I pissed off," the tape said.

"Damn, am I pissed off!" I yelled, flinging yet another pair, these teal.

"I can't believe you bought trendy teal socks," the tape said, "Don't you know they'll be out of style in six months?"

"Shut up!" I screamed, hurling a pair of heavy woolen camping socks directly at the tape player, knocking it over.

"That's good!" the voice said from the floor where the player had landed. "Vent that anger! Beat on a pillow! Let's hear a primal scream!"

"Arrgh!" I yelled, shredding a pillow with my bare

hands, feathers flying wildly about.

Suddenly it was quiet. I looked around me. Clothes were strewn everywhere. Nickels and dimes covered the rug. Posters, hit by socks, hung askew. Feathers continued to float down slowly.

I looked at the tape player. Side one was over. I flipped the tape and read the title of side two: *Cleaning up the emotional mess of a break up.* I put it in and pressed PLAY.

illustration by Noreen Stevens

BOOKS BY
LAUGH LINES PRESS

**Who Cares If It's a Choice? Snappy Answers
to 101 Nosy, Intrusive and Highly Personal
Questions about Lesbians and Gays**
$7.50 U.S. / $9.00 CANADA
Ellen Orleans; Explore the world of bear clubs,
gaydar, ice-pick lesbians, and the Dinah Shore
Golf Classic. Real-life homosexuality at its
funniest!

**Can't Keep A Straight Face:
A Lesbian Looks and Laughs at Life**
$7.50 U.S. / $9.00 CANADA
Ellen Orleans; illustrations by Noreen Stevens.
Essays about softball, the religious right, coming out, breaking up, saving the earth and
more!

Stand Back, I Think I'm Gonna Laugh. . .
$7.95 U.S. / $9.50 CANADA
Rina Piccolo; Terrific kick-in-the-brain
cartoons about sex, life, car phones, bad
hair, the Catholic Church and much more!

Men! Ha!
$7.50 U.S./$9.00 CANADA
Stephanie Piro; Marvelously funny
cartoons about life, love and romance.
Great for women who love to laugh at men.

After Mike walked out, she decided
to give up Men and raise chickens.
 Chickens didn't stay out all night,
or come home drunk, or sleep with
your best girlfriend...
 And if they did... you could cut
off their heads and eat them...

The Butches of Madison County
Ellen Orleans
$7.95 U.S.A./$9.00 CANADA

Can true love blossom between a wandering lesbian writer seeking wisdom from her past and a straight Iowa farmwife looking for a future (not to mention a life)?

Find out when Billie, a post-menopausal heroine for the '90's and Patsy, the butchiest straight women you'll ever meet, come together (literally) for five unbelievable romatic days that must last a lifetime.

Rude Girls and Dangerous Women
$8.95 U.S./$11.50 CANADA
Jennifer Camper

Of *Rude Girls and Dangerous Women*, Alison
Bechdel says: Sick of Lesbian Chic? Wistful
for the days when queers were queers and not
domestic partners? In Jen Camper's universe
of sexy, sweaty, swaggering switch-blade-
wielding women, the only law is: Dykes Rule.

Weenie-Toons:
Women Cartoonists Mock Cocks: $4.50
If you've ever laughed at a penis, this is the book
for you. Diane DiMassa, Kris Kovick,
Alison Bechdel, Noreen Stevens, Lynda Barry,
Andrea Natalie and more!

As always, please support your local
feminist-friendly bookstore whenever possible.

——— TO ORDER BY MAIL ———

addition to the price of each book,
please include $1.00 for postage and handling
at book rate delivery.

Make payment to Laugh Lines Press and mail to
P.O. Box 259, Bala Cynwyd, PA 19004

DYKE ON TRIKE, 1962

ABOUT THE AUTHOR

Since completing her last book, *Can't Keep a Straight Face*, Ellen has led a blessed life, although she frequently fails to notice that fact.

After a 12-state summer book tour, she returned to Colorado to find Amendment 2 on its way to defeat, her incipient love relationship still intact and an affordable apartment newly-materialized.

She continues to run the Macintosh lab at The Naropa Institute, explore Denver's Botanical Gardens with her lover and seek spiritual truth where ever it might be. Most recently, she found it in a dish of raspberry chocolate mousse ice cream.